Seaside Devotions

A collection of devotionals
to inspire and uplift

by Sherron Lane

Proceeds from the sale of this book will be used
for the Kingdom work for widows and orphans.

All scripture quotations, unless otherwise indicated, are taken from the Holy Bible,
New International Version®, NIV®.
Copyright ©1973, 1978, 1984 by Biblica, Inc.™
Used by permission of Zondervan. All rights reserved worldwide.
www.zondervan.com

Scripture quotations marked NLT are taken from the Holy Bible, New Living Translation,
copyright 1996, 2004. Used by permission of Tyndale House Publishers, Inc., Wheaton, Illinois 60189.
All rights reserved.

Scripture quotations marked NKJV™ are taken from the New King James Version®.
Copyright © 1982 by Thomas Nelson, Inc. Used by permission.
All rights reserved.

Scripture quotations taken from the Amplified® Bible,
Copyright © 1954, 1958, 1962, 1964, 1965, 1987 by The Lockman Foundation.
Used by permission.
www.Lockman.org

Copyright © 2011 Sherron Lane
All rights reserved.

ISBN: 145386394X
ISBN: 978-1453863947

SEASIDE DEVOTIONS
A New Kingdom Publishing Book / February 2011
www.NewKingdomPublishing.com

Printed in the U.S.A.

Cover and book design by Deanna Grant, www.GrantDesignStudio.com
Editing by Kay King
Cover photograph by Jock Bethune

Foreward

Seaside Devotions is one of my favorite devotional books. It comes across in a very laid back way to bring peace to your heart and soul.

It is very simple to read as it will minister to each person who reads it. It's a daily read and will help everyone who reads it have a more intimate walk with the Lord. I highly recommend this book to every believer.

Joan Hunter, D Div.
Apostle/Author/Evangelist
President Joan Hunter Ministries

Introduction

It is my honor to share my seaside devotions with you. Every day I continue to be awed by God's glorious creation as I listen to the waves lap at the shore, observe His creatures on which He keeps watchful eyes and see the sun make its daily path across the sky.

May God speak to your heart through these devotions as He has spoken to mine. I have included journal pages after each devotion for you to record your thoughts and prayers.

It is my hope that these devotions will inspire you to take time each day to be still and hear the voice of God. It is my prayer that He will give you strength and courage to be all He has called you to be as you meditate daily on His Word.

— *Sherron Lane*

As I walked the seaside with Jesus, I found a quiet place to sit on the beach. The warm glow of the sun hit my face as I listened for His voice.

We must take time to come aside and still ourselves before our Heavenly Father to hear what He has to say! How else will we know which way to go, except we wait for Him to give us direction! We must be still before we move, or we will be moved by our own thoughts and plans—not His! Our Father knows what is ahead and will tell us if we are willing to "wait for Him."

How many times have you moved ahead with your plans and ideas that seemed good, sounded great at the time, only to fail at the end of the course? Our Father says if we commit our ways to Him, He will direct our paths in life. So, to be sure we are on the right journey, we need to get our instructions from the Director of our paths. He will keep us out of trouble and show us the way to go if we are willing to make the sacrifice of time to be with Him.

Before you rush into your day, take the time to "wait before Him." Hear what He is telling you today! See if your path doesn't become more peaceful and straight! He knows the way to go!

Trust in the LORD with all your heart and lean not on your own understanding; in all your ways acknowledge him and he will make your paths straight.

— Proverbs 3:5-6

As I walked the seaside with Jesus, I watched the dolphins playing along the shoreline. They were free to enjoy the ocean and not worry about the future.

What are you doing in your life? Are your thoughts on your Heavenly Father and all He has given you to enjoy, or are you thinking about the problems or issues of life?

Our continual focus should be seeking our Father and His will for our lives. Such a mind-set will protect us from scattering our energy to the winds of life. We all have issues and problems to deal with daily, but our Heavenly Father says for us not to be anxious about what we are to eat, to wear or any of these things... and that is exactly what He meant. Because He loves us, He provides us with all things to live our lives here on the earth.

So, today as you walk your seashore of life, think about the gifts He has put in your life here on the earth and how He has provided all you ever will need. We have a free will, and daily we can make the choice to follow Him or follow the way of the world. Rejoice today and be free—just like the dolphins. Live and enjoy the abundant life!

> *"The thief comes only to steal and kill and destroy;*
> *I have come that they may have life, and have it to the full."*
>
> *— John 10:10*

As I walked the seaside with Jesus, I felt as though the waves were taking me to a new place in time. They were crisp and white—like a fresh wind from the throne room. The ocean seemed brisk, sharp and alive! It was as though Jesus was running with me, saying, "Let's run faster. Let's try to catch the waves."

God has a direction for each of us... a plan with a purpose. We must be prepared to run quickly as He comes alongside us. He gives us the visions, the dreams and the strategies with which to run. It is time to fly! It is time to take our assignments seriously, and trust God to provide. How different life would be if each of us would accept the responsibility to hear and heed what the Holy Spirit is saying.

Remind yourself what your dreams and visions are—write them down and put them before you. "Then the LORD replied: 'Write down the revelation and make it plain on tablets...'" (Habakkuk 2:2). "For as he thinketh in his heart, so is he..." (Proverbs 23:7 KJV). It is important we determine where we want our minds to go and what we want our minds to think. We make that choice every minute of the day.

Let's decide to seek Him, and get the wisdom provided for us in the "manual of life"... the Bible. There you will find the answers you need to live a life of success! We can't go to others all the time and expect them to give us the answers for our lives. We must go to the Master, and He will answer us through His Word.

Direct me in the path of your commands, for there I find delight.
— *Psalm 119:35*

As I walked the seaside with Jesus, I realized the depth of the ocean is far more than we could ever fathom. Jesus did not say how deep we are to step into the water. The depth of the water into which we sail depends upon how completely we have cut our ties to the shore—the greatness of our needs and anxieties about our future.

We are to sail into the depth of God's Word, which the Holy Spirit will open to us, with profound yet crystal-clear meaning. The deep waters of the Holy Spirit always are accessible because they always are flowing. God wants to touch what you do, but you must be in motion before He can bless it! God will not steer a parked car. He is waiting for us to take the position He has assigned us. It is time for us to move forward!

Sometimes we aren't willing to take responsibility of seeking God's guidance for ourselves. We want to look for an easy way out, and let someone else tell us what to do. God wants a personal relationship with each of His children. He wants us to hear Him for ourselves and to follow the leading of the Holy Spirit.

How different life would be for each of us if we would accept the responsibility to hear and heed what the Holy Spirit is saying to us. We could avoid so many trials and difficulties if we just follow that leading!

But when he, the Spirit of truth, comes, he will guide you into all truth. He will not speak on his own; he will speak only what he hears, and he will tell you what is yet to come.

— John 16:13

As I walked the seaside with Jesus, there was a tiny sandpiper following me along the ocean. It was as though we were walking as one along God's beautiful beach, enjoying the fellowship of our Father.

As God's children, we have a covenant that provides everything we need on this earth. It is so critical we pay attention with whom we enter into covenant…in our business and in our daily walk of life.

How do we expect to be successful when we covenant with those who are walking in darkness? When we choose to form a covenant with those who are walking in darkness, we take on everything that is in that person's business and personal life. We are to be wise in the relationships we form. For example, know who the person is; know what their business is. This is the wisdom God gives us when He states in His Word to be equally yoked.

Think about your relationships before you form them. Do what God says, and be selective when you make these choices. It will save you a lot of heartache and pain if you choose to walk with light and not darkness. Seems simple, but we have a tendency to make choices thinking we can change others. That is the job of the Holy Spirit—not ours. So, choose wisely and live victoriously today.

> *Do not be yoked together with unbelievers. For what do righteousness and wickedness have in common? Or what fellowship can light have with darkness?*
>
> — *2 Corinthians 6:14*

As I walked the seaside with Jesus, I wanted to hurry along. I felt the Holy Spirit gently speak to me and say, "Slow down."

Human nature tends to want everything right now. We are always in a hurry. Most of us get impatient when we miss a turn in a revolving door! When we pray for our dreams to come to pass, we want them to be fulfilled immediately. We have to understand God has an appointed time to answer our prayers and to bring our dreams to pass. The truth is, no matter how quickly we want something, no matter how much we pray and plead with God, most likely it's not going to change His appointed time.

Sometimes we don't understand God's timing. We live upset, frustrated lives and wonder when God is going to do something. "God, when are you going to change my husband? When are you going to bring me a mate? When is my business going to take off? When are my dreams going to come to pass?"

Consider this... if you know you are going to have to wait anyway, why not make a decision to enjoy your life while you are waiting? Why not be happy while God is in the process of changing things? After all, there is nothing you can do to hurry the process. Slow down and be happy! Trust God to bring these things to pass, and enjoy your walk with Him.

> .... *Though it linger, wait for it; it will certainly come and will not delay.*
>
> — *Habakkuk 2:3*

As I walked the seaside with Jesus, I watched the tiny sandpipers chasing the waves to get their food. They never stopped swiftly running and searching along the shoreline. They were determined to succeed in finding their food.

Do you have the joy of the Lord in your life today? Do you run freely, trusting Him to take care of all your needs? That is how He wants us to live—to know He is there, taking care of our every need. We can live without the stress of worry by being responsible and by not carrying the weight of the world on our backs—like so many of us do.

Every morning, when you get up, set your mind for success. Almost like a magnet, we constantly draw to us what we think. It becomes a battlefield in our minds. If we dwell on depressing and negative thoughts, we will be depressed and negative. If we think positive, happy and joyful thoughts, our lives will reflect those thoughts and will attract other upbeat, positive people. Our lives follow our thoughts.

Our thoughts also affect our emotions. We will feel exactly the way we think. You cannot expect to feel happy unless you think happy thoughts. On the other hand, it is impossible to remain discouraged unless you first think discouraging thoughts. Success and failure in life begins in our minds. So, today as you walk your seashore of life, keep your thoughts focused on happy, uplifting things. See what joy your day will bring.

> "…. This is what the LORD says to you:
> 'Do not be afraid or discouraged because of this vast army.
> For the battle is not yours, but God's.'"
>
> — *2 Chronicles 20:15*

As I walked the seaside with Jesus, I was reminded that our lives are but a vapor on the earth. We need to make the most of every day we live, and enjoy it to the fullest. You might make mistakes, and things may not always go your way. But, you can make a decision to not allow what does or does not happen to steal your joy and ruin your day.

As we move forward, we must keep our focus on Him. We have the freedom and ability to choose what is our focus every moment of the day! We are the only creation on the earth who has been given this ability, which proves we are created in His magnificent image!

Be encouraged by the assurance that God will never leave you or forsake you. God tells us when He is your delight, He will give you the desires of your heart. He has placed those desires in your heart, and He surely will fulfill them! So, do not give up and lose heart.

Let the goal of this day be to bring every thought captive to Jesus. Bring every wandering thought back into the presence of our King. In His presence every fear, concern, worry and anxious thought shrinks into nothing. Judgmental thoughts are transformed into thoughts of love and compassion.

> *You will keep in perfect peace him whose mind is steadfast, because he trusts in you.*
>
> — *Isaiah 26:3*

As I walked the seaside with Jesus, I watched a sandpiper chase the little crabs in the sand. He never gave up until he had caught his food. He became a conqueror!

How about you? Are you more than a conqueror? Notice the Apostle Paul did not say we will become conquerors; he says we are more than conquerors—right now! If you will start acting like it, talking like it and seeing yourself as more than a conqueror, you will live a prosperous and victorious life. The price already has been paid for you to have joy, peace and happiness. That's part of the package God has made available to you.

We have to walk in faith, not fear. We have to believe He is for us. And if He is for us, no one can be against us. He always will keep us strong as long as we keep our eyes on Him. Focus only on what He can do—not what we in our own strength can do!

Today, start looking through eyes of faith, seeing yourself rising to new levels. See yourself prospering, and keep that image in your heart and mind. You may be living in poverty at the moment, but don't ever let poverty live in you. The Bible teaches that God takes pleasure in prospering His children. As His children prosper spiritually, physically and materially, their increase brings God pleasure! Through Jesus, you can become more than a conqueror in this life!

Now if we are children, then we are heirs—heirs of God and co-heirs with Christ, if indeed we share in his sufferings in order that we may also share in his glory.

— *Romans 8:17*

$\mathcal{A}$s I walked the seaside with Jesus, I was reminded that every day we are the ambassadors of Christ on the earth. Every day we should be speaking His blessings to those around us—just as His creatures speak to me every day on the beach as they play in His mighty ocean.

Often the people who do not know God will have difficulty understanding why you place your confidence in someone you cannot see. They even may fear what they do not comprehend and endeavor to discourage or discredit you.

You never should be afraid of representing God. You are growing daily in the character of the One you represent—each day resembling Him more and more. However, always remember that as you stand for God, He is the One Who empowers and protects you. It is His duty to defend His name. He will show Himself to you in a way that both validates your trust in Him and shows the one who opposes you His love.

Seek others who offer you positive, sustaining words of faith. You, in turn, can encourage others. Be that friend who is uplifting and a blessing to those around you. If God loves us like this, we certainly ought to love each other. No one has seen God—ever. But if we love one another, God dwells deeply within us, and His love becomes complete in us—perfect love!

We love because he first loved us.

— *1 John 4:19*

As I walked the seaside with Jesus, the beach was quiet—no crowds—just Jesus and me! It was such a still and quiet time.

We sometimes get lost in the noises surrounding us daily. There are so many voices crying out for our time from the moment we awake. The job we have, our children, our spouse and the day-to-day demands that are not on the schedule, begin to scream for our attention.

We seem to somehow lose our way because we do not hear His voice amidst the turmoil of this life. He says for us to be still and know that He is God. That tells me we have to make the effort to come away to hear Him; otherwise, we will not know what He is leading us to do! We can become confused, afraid, depressed, oppressed and lost—wanderers in the wilderness and not effective here on earth!

Jesus set an example for us. Remember how often He went to be alone with God? There was a powerful purpose behind His command to go into your room, shut the door and pray. Today, make an effort to be still, hear His voice and let Him do the leading! He has been waiting for you—to speak into your life. He is God, and He does speak to us when we allow Him.

> "For I know the plans I have for you," declares the LORD, "plans to prosper you and not to harm you, plans to give you hope and a future. Then you will call upon me and come and pray to me, and I will listen to you. You will seek me and find me when you seek me with all your heart."
>
> — *Jeremiah 29:11-13*

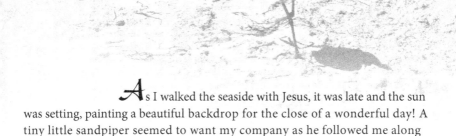

As I walked the seaside with Jesus, it was late and the sun was setting, painting a beautiful backdrop for the close of a wonderful day! A tiny little sandpiper seemed to want my company as he followed me along the shore.

Isn't that the way we are at times... watching a perfect day and just wanting to share it with a friend? It is so comforting to know we always have that friend to share with us no matter where we go! It is Jesus—He is our friend. He is always there to share whatever we feel, think or say—no matter what may be going on in our lives. We may be hurting or at times confused about the next step in our lives, but He is there—ready to walk beside us and to lead the way!

When He becomes the center of our lives, He is there every day—when there are storms and when there is peace. What a blessing to know we are never, ever going to have to be alone—no matter what! Like the tiny sandpiper that wanted to share the walk with a friend today, He is there to share your walk with you. Let Him be that friend Who walks daily with you, and see what a joy your life can be. He is the "true friend" Who will never leave you or forsake you!

So, today as you walk your seashore of life, make sure the one thing you have in place is your relationship with Him. He is the sure thing that you can count on every day. Put Him at the center of your heart today!

> *"Be strong and courageous. Do not be afraid or terrified because of them, for the LORD your God goes with you; he will never leave you nor forsake you."*
>
> — *Deuteronomy 31:6*

As I walked the seaside with Jesus, it was amazing to feel my body move and be coordinated as the Creator has designed it. I was reminded my body is the temple of the Holy Spirit.

The mind is so much like the body—what you put into it makes a difference in how it works. If you eat a lot of junk food, your health deteriorates. Similarly, if you put negative thoughts into your mind, they act like a poison—killing your ability to have faith or to live a life pleasing to God.

Paul's admonishment to the Philippians is for us as well. We are to fill our minds with things that are true, noble, reputable, authentic, compelling and gracious. Such things affect your outlook and empower you to be the best you can be. As long as we are in this world, there always will be something enticing us to worry or doubt. We have the choice to refuse this temptation by continually communicating with the Father. Awareness of the Father's presence fills our minds with light and peace, leaving no room for fear or worry! This awareness lifts us above every circumstance we encounter!

So, today as you walk your seashore of life, feed your mind with thoughts of God and His Word. His nourishment will never leave you feeling empty, hungry or afraid.

> *Finally, brothers, whatever is true, whatever is noble, whatever is right, whatever is pure, whatever is lovely, whatever is admirable—if anything is excellent or praiseworthy— think about such things.*
>
> *— Philippians 4:8*

$\mathcal{A}$s I walked the seaside with Jesus, the dolphins were playing in the water... jumping high out of the water... higher than I had seen them before! What a wonderful sight! It reminded me that Jesus wants to take us higher in our faith daily!

After the two blind men told Jesus they believed, He was able to heal them. "Then he touched their eyes, and said, 'According to your faith will it be done to you;' and their sight was restored..." (Matthew 9:29-30). Notice, it was their faith that brought them the healing.

What are you believing? Are you believing to go higher in life, to rise above your obstacles, to live in good health, abundance, healing and victory? You will become what you believe. You don't have to figure out how God is going to solve your problems or bring it to pass. That is His responsibility. Your job is to believe.

We are created to be faith creatures, not worry creatures. It seems to me we all know how to worry—but not so much how to believe and trust our Father to work all things together in our lives for our good. Faith is what moves our Father, not worry. Relax and believe He is for you, because He is bringing that plan into being! So, today as you walk your seashore of life, trust Him. Be at peace today!

> *He replied, "Because you have so little faith. I tell you the truth, if you have faith as small as a mustard seed, you can say to this mountain, 'Move from here to there' and it will move. Nothing will be impossible for you."*
>
> *— Matthew 17:20*

As I walked the seaside with Jesus, I felt the love of God submerge my soul along the quiet beach. It is amazing how, at moments of solitude, you can feel the presence and love of God in such a tangible way.

The moment you accepted Jesus, all of His goodness, grace, joy and power were given to you. This may be difficult to grasp if you have been reminded of failings or previously have not viewed yourself in such a positive light. However, this is not about you, but about the effect God has on you.

It will come as no surprise to you that much of your success is dependent upon your focus. It may astonish you to know on what Jesus focused. What brought Him victory was joy! He was able to face the Cross by looking past it—to the wonderful and joyous prospect of offering you a relationship with God by doing God's will.

Every day we make a choice as to what thoughts we think. Everyday we can choose to be grateful for what He has done. On what do you choose to focus? Do you choose to think on the world's thoughts of worry, stress, disaster, confusion or His thoughts of goodness, hope, mercy and grace? It is your choice... choose His thoughts today!

> *For as he thinks in his heart, so is he. As one who reckons, he says to you, eat and drink, yet his heart is not with you [but is grudging the cost].*
>
> *— Proverbs 23:7 (AMP)*

As I walked the seaside with Jesus, I started one way and then felt led to walk the opposite way on the beach. God let me choose the way I chose to walk.

Understand this: God will help you in life, but you cast the deciding vote. If you choose to stay focused on negative elements in your life—if you are focused on what you can't do and what you don't have—then by your own choice, you are agreeing to be defeated. You are conspiring with the devil by allowing destructive thoughts, words, actions and attitudes to dominate your life.

Our expectations have tremendous power in our lives. We don't always get what we deserve in life, and we usually get no more than we expect. We receive what we believe. Unfortunately, this principle works as strongly in the negative as it does in the positive. Many people expect defeat, failure and mediocrity—and, they usually get it.

But you, my friend, can believe for good things just as easily as you can expect the worst. The key is to expect good things from God. When you encounter tough times, ask God for wisdom and change what you expect. Even if the bottom falls out of your life, your attitude should be: "God, I know You are going to use this for my good. I believe You are going to bring me out stronger than ever before."

> *"'.....If you do not stand firm in your faith, you will not stand at all.'"*
>
> — *Isaiah 7:9*

As I walked the seaside with Jesus, I started one way and then felt led to walk the opposite way on the beach. God let me choose the way I chose to walk.

Understand this: God will help you in life, but you cast the deciding vote. If you choose to stay focused on negative elements in your life—if you are focused on what you can't do and what you don't have—then by your own choice, you are agreeing to be defeated. You are conspiring with the devil by allowing destructive thoughts, words, actions and attitudes to dominate your life.

Our expectations have tremendous power in our lives. We don't always get what we deserve in life, and we usually get no more than we expect. We receive what we believe. Unfortunately, this principle works as strongly in the negative as it does in the positive. Many people expect defeat, failure and mediocrity—and, they usually get it.

But you, my friend, can believe for good things just as easily as you can expect the worst. The key is to expect good things from God. When you encounter tough times, ask God for wisdom and change what you expect. Even if the bottom falls out of your life, your attitude should be: "God, I know You are going to use this for my good. I believe You are going to bring me out stronger than ever before."

> *"'.....If you do not stand firm in your faith, you will not stand at all.'"*
>
> — *Isaiah 7:9*

As I walked the seaside with Jesus, I found a sand dollar that was beautiful and fully formed. It was as though my Father laid it on the beach just waiting for me... such favor from above.

When you live favor-minded, you'll begin to see God's goodness everyday in ordinary details—at the grocery store, at the ball field, at the mall, at work or on the beach. You may be out for lunch when you "just happen" to bump into someone you have been wanting to meet. That is not a coincidence. That is the favor of God causing you to be at the right place at the right time. When these encounters happen, be grateful. Be sure to thank God for His favor. Never take God's favor for granted.

Many people nowadays are blatantly and unashamedly living for themselves. Society teaches us to look out for number one. Ironically, this selfish attitude condemns us to living shallow, unrewarding lives. No matter how much we acquire for ourselves, we never are satisfied.

God is a giver. If you want to experience a new level of God's joy, if you want Him to pour out His blessings and favor into your life, then you must learn to be a giver and not a taker. Wherever you are, find someone to bless—just as your Father has taught you. So, today as you walk your seashore of life, remember, you are blessed to be a blessing in all the earth!

You gave me life and showed me kindness,
and in your providence watched over my spirit.

— *Job 10:12*

As I walked the seaside with Jesus, I again was amazed at the beauty of the ocean rolling onto the shore. I couldn't help but wonder how anyone could look at God's beautiful ocean and not believe in Him.

Knowing Him gives you peace that never leaves you. He is able to hold us steady even in the storms of life, just as He holds the ocean within its boundaries! God wants you to have a good life—a life filled with love, joy, peace and fulfillment. This doesn't mean it always will be easy, but it does mean it always will be good. "And we know that all things work together for good to those who love God, to those who are the called according to His purpose" (Romans 8:28 NKJV).

Be encouraged, my friend. No one can take away what God has given to you. His complete, unconditional love and approval are yours forever. Rejoice and delight yourself in Him as you enjoy the seaside He created, wherever that may be.

> *He has made everything beautiful in its time.*
> *He has also set eternity in the hearts of men; yet they cannot*
> *fathom what God has done from beginning to end.*
>
> *— Ecclesiastes 3:11*

As I walked the seaside with Jesus, it was gray and gloomy. It seemed to be a battle to think about the blue sky above because I could not see it. I chose to think about the sun that was shining above the dark clouds—not on the gray sky I could see.

We all make a choice every day. We all get knocked down occasionally and get discouraged, but we need not remain there. We can choose our thoughts. No one can make us think a certain way. If you're not happy, no one else is forcing you to be unhappy. If you're negative and have a bad attitude, no one is coercing you to be sarcastic or sullen. You decide what you will entertain in your mind.

Simply because the enemy plants a negative, discouraging thought in your brain, doesn't mean you have to nurture it and help it grow. If you do, though, that thought will affect your emotions, your attitudes and eventually your actions. You will be much more prone to discouragement and depression. If you continue pondering that negative thought, it will sap the energy and strength right out of you. Choose to believe God is greater than your problems.

When you start your busy day, take the time to find a quiet spot to say to Him how very grateful you are. Tell Him how thankful you are to have a loving Father Who is always looking out for you. See if it doesn't make a difference in your day.

Your attitude should be the same as that of Christ Jesus:

— *Philippians 2:5*

As I walked the seaside with Jesus, I watched a little mound of sand that had once been a beautiful sandcastle being wiped out by the waves. It made me think of one word that completely wipes out our past mistakes. That one word is "forgiveness."

Did you ever wish you could start over? Probably all of us have longed for another chance in some area of our lives. Maybe we wouldn't have done things differently, just perhaps more or less. The truth is, we can't go backward, only forward into uncharted territory. To sit in our sorrow would lead to misery, and that is not what our Father in Heaven wants for us!

If we had changed any part of our lives, there is no guarantee things would have turned out differently. We just have to trust the God of the Universe, Who directs the outcome of all things. He will do that which ultimately needs to be done. We know that He, through the tool of forgiveness, will make our paths clean again.

So, today as you walk your seashore of life, live with no regrets. Ask for forgiveness, and move forward trusting God as your pilot! He is the One Who knows the way!

Rid yourselves of all the offenses you have committed, and get a new heart and a new spirit. Why will you die, O house of Israel?

— *Ezekiel 18:31*

As I walked the seaside with Jesus, I felt like the whole world was in love. I felt the love of the Father wrapped around me as I viewed His incredible creation. The sun was rising out of the ocean; the day was coming to life. An eagle soared above the waves. I wanted to share this love with everyone I met.

You have the opportunity every day to show Jesus to the world by walking in His love, the love of the Father. He was first revealed and expressed in His Son, Jesus, and is now manifested in you.

Our human love generally is described as a feeling. Often it is based on fleeting, momentary passions. Outwardly, even minor things can affect human love's disposition. It looks inward to its own interests. Human love grows harder and less trusting with each negative experience. However, God's love is different from human love. His love is not an emotion. It is a deliberate, consistent action that is given unconditionally. His love is not moved by circumstances, because He looks outwardly to our best interests.

The world is looking for something real, something tangible and is looking for love. God is the source of all love. God is making His appeal to the world through you; therefore, love others with God's kind of love…agape love. His love will spill out onto those He brings into your life, and you will show His love on the earth.

> *"By this all men will know that you are my disciples, if you love one another."*
>
> — *John 13:35*

As I walked the seaside with Jesus, the ocean was calm and smooth as glass. It reminded me of the peace of God. I was compelled to stop and rest and just enjoy the view.

Two painters were once asked to paint a picture illustrating their own idea of rest. The first painter chose for his scene a quiet, lonely lake nestled among mountains far away. The second one, using swift, broad strokes on his canvas, painted a strong, thundering waterfall. Beneath the falls grew a fragile birch tree, bending over the foam. On its branches, nearly wet with the spray from the falls, sat a robin on its nest.

The first painting was simply a picture of stagnation and inactivity. The second, however, depicted rest.

Outwardly, Christ endured one of the most troubled lives ever lived. Storms and turmoil, turmoil and storms... wave after wave broke over Him until His worn body was laid in the Tomb. During this time of stormy turmoil, His inner life was as smooth as a sea of glass, and a great calm was always there.

So, today as you walk your seashore of life, remember, rest is not some holy feeling that comes upon us in church. It is a state of calm rising from a heart deeply and firmly established in God.

> *"Peace I leave with you; my peace I give you.*
> *I do not give to you as the world gives.*
> *Do not let your hearts be troubled and do not be afraid."*
> *— John 14:27*

As I walked the seaside with Jesus, I always have been amazed at how the sandpipers never fret about finding food or provision. They just run about the beach, finding everything they need. I think of how we worry so much about our own provision.

There was a time in Israel when the rains stopped flowing for three years. Because of that, there was no wheat in the fields to make flour or olives in the trees to make oil. It was a very difficult time for everyone, particularly for one widow who was especially committed to serving God. Yet God made sure the widow and her son had enough to eat because they did all He asked.

We are anxious, worry over things and carry burdens He never meant for us to carry. We forget we have the King of the Universe with all knowledge, all power and all peace available to us. It is as simple as just asking and acknowledging His very presence in our lives.

So, as you walk your seashore of life, do not fear lean days. Rather, rejoice that His provision never ends. There is more than enough. God always provides for those who love and do as He says. Obey Him. You will be amazed how He keeps the flour and oil flowing.

> *"For this is what the LORD, the God of Israel, says: 'The jar of flour will not be used up and the jug of oil will not run dry until the day the LORD gives rain on the land.'"*
>
> *— 1 Kings 17:14*

As I walked the seaside with Jesus, I thought of how His forgiveness is such an amazing gift to each of us. I thought how freely I can walk along the beach and know I am loved by my Heavenly Father.

The depth of Jesus' compassion is mind-boggling. As others wrongly accused and crucified Him, He recognized they did not know what they were doing. Jesus asked God to forgive them. I am sure you have had people like that in your own life. When people hurt you, I truly believe they do not understand what they are doing. They may think they understand, but they could not possibly comprehend the full ramifications of hurting someone whom God loves.

It is an astounding, poignant picture—one that should resonate within your soul as you read this. What a comfort to know that even though we fail, He never looks at our failures if we repent and ask for forgiveness. He wipes the slate clean. We don't have to carry the sins and mistakes of yesterday with us throughout our lives.

So, today as you walk your seashore of life, forgive as Jesus did—with compassion and understanding. In doing so, you set yourself and the one who hurt you free. Make the choice to live today in freedom as one loved and forgiven by Jesus.

> *"For if you forgive men when they sin against you, your heavenly Father will also forgive you. But if you do not forgive men their sins, your Father will not forgive your sins."*
>
> *— Matthew 6:14-15*

As I walked the seaside with Jesus, more than ever I heard His call to serve. Have you come to a fork in your road of life? Do you feel God's call to serve? Do you recognize His voice and know it is He? Simply wait on Him and say, "Yes."

Don't ponder the why or what-ifs...neither question your abilities as we often tend to do. Don't worry about timing or the future. God's calling is sure. We don't have to worry about making a way. If it is His will, He will work all things out in His own perfect way and in His own timing. He calls us through, around, over and under to serve. Be assured, God will give you what you need in order to serve when you need it.

When the mighty winds blow, He will miraculously place them at your back. When the floods begin to rage, He may tell you to keep paddling in faith while He calms the seas. Our continual focus should be seeking our Father and His will for our lives. Such a mind-set will protect us from scattering our energy to the winds.

God teaches us to trust Him with one step at a time. So, today as you walk your seashore of life, praise Him for the directions He is giving you. Praise Him for always being trustworthy to take you to the vision and to the victory He has prepared for your life. Join in His activity, and you will have just the right gifts for the task He assigns you to accomplish.

The one who calls you is faithful and he will do it.

— *1 Thessalonians 5:24*

$\mathcal{A}$s I walked the seaside with Jesus, my thoughts went to Joseph, my favorite Bible character, and how he was mistreated in his youth by his brothers.

Joseph's brothers were cruel. They sold him to traveling merchants. They set about a chain of events in Joseph's life that brought him to a position of prominence where he profoundly provided for people during a challenging time.

Joseph could have been bitter about his difficult life, but he realized God had a plan. Joseph understood God placed him in a position to help others. Joseph forgave his brothers and also was gracious to them.

There is an abundance of discouragement coming from the world. You may be distraught over the actions of others. However, you can be certain, when you see God's plan unfold, you will find He has transformed everything into good for the blessings of others. You have the great privilege of bringing encouragement to others by being positive in a negative world.

So, today as you walk your seashore of life, I encourage you to ask God to help you choose words and actions that will bring positive changes to the lives of others—and in your own life, as well.

"But God sent me ahead of you to preserve for you a remnant on earth and to save your lives by a great deliverance."

— *Genesis 45:7*

$\mathcal{A}$s I walked the seaside with Jesus, my thoughts were focused on the dreams in my heart. They seemed to be much bigger than anything I could ever achieve on my own. I thought of the things God asks us to do in our day-to-day lives.

I have found He seems to never ask us to do things that are humanly possible. He does not fill our hearts with goals we easily can achieve on our own. Instead, God gives us dreams far greater and more wonderful than we ever could aspire to on our own. God-given dreams can be accomplished only if He actively is involved in our lives.

Why? Because God wants you to know the good that happens to you is from Him. That way you will rely on Him and His power and resources—not man's. He is bringing the hopes that burn in you into being.

No matter how long you have believed in God, you will have moments of weakness. You will be tempted to believe it is impossible to surmount what is ahead. Your best remedy is to focus on the One Who is absolutely true and consistently faithful. God perfectly guides and equips you for the journey, keeping you from swerving away from your purposes.

So, today as you walk your seashore of life, trust Him to make all those impossible dreams come true. He put those dreams into your heart and mind. He is the God of the impossible!

> *Jesus looked at them and said, "With man this is impossible, but with God all things are possible."*
>
> — *Matthew 19:26*

As I walked the seaside with Jesus, I found a seashell that was covered with debris. But once I washed it off, it was beautiful. Sometimes we have to remind ourselves that with God we always have value, even though we may seem to be tarnished and worn.

Imagine I am handing you a new, crisp, one-hundred-dollar bill. Would you want it? Probably so! If I crumpled it, you'd still want it. And if I threw it on the ground and stomped on it until the picture on the bill was barely perceptible, you'd still want it, because you know that a beat-up one-hundred-dollar bill is still worth a hundred dollars.

That's the way God sees each of us. We all go through challenges and struggles. Sometimes we feel like that crumpled and soiled one-hundred-dollar bill. But, in fact, we will never lose our value. It has been thoughtfully placed in us by the Creator of the Universe.

Be encouraged, my friend. No one can take away what God has given to you. His complete love and approval are yours forever. So, rejoice and delight yourself in Him as you enjoy the seaside He created—wherever that may be. Remember, God loves you forever!

> *...neither height nor depth, nor anything else in all creation, will be able to separate us from the love of God that is in Christ Jesus our Lord.*
>
> — *Romans 8:39*

As I walked the seaside with Jesus, the air was crisp and cool. It touched my face and reminded me each day is a new day! Every day started with a pure heart—free of anger and unforgiveness—an exciting new chance to live life to the fullest!

Scripture instructs us to put on a fresh new attitude every morning, especially in our relationships. Don't let little things build up. Do not harbor unforgiveness and resentment. Don't allow bad attitudes to develop, even those that may seem insignificant to you. Over a period of time, bitter attitudes can grow. They can cause you major problems. You have to do your best to keep your own heart free and clean; otherwise, anger, bitterness and resentment will affect your relationships.

We can walk victoriously every day no matter what the enemy tries to bring against us. We are the head and not the tail, above and not beneath! We have victory as we stay focused on God's Word, not the words of the enemy!

Each night before you sleep, forgive the people who have hurt you, and let go of your disappointments and setbacks. Each new morning, receive God's mercy and forgiveness for the mistakes you have made. Focus on your possibilities. Focus on what you can change rather than what you cannot change.

"In your anger do not sin. Do not let the sun go down while you are still angry, and do not give the devil a foothold."

— *Ephesians 4:26-27*

As I walked the seaside with Jesus, the sound of the ocean lapped gently against the beach. It seems on these days the voice of the Lord is much louder than the days it is raging against the sand!

I thought of the verse, " 'Be still, and know that I am God...' " (Psalm 46:10). To have God's direction for our lives, we all have to get to a place where we can quiet the voices of the world, and hear what the Lord is saying. This is truly a challenge we all face because the enemy will keep us occupied with "busy things" to do and will keep us from hearing the small, still voice of the Lord.

We can't just wake up and fall into our day without His leading because of a rushed schedule, and yet, many of us do. I have been there, done that, and when I do, my day ends up being scrambled because it started that way... without His leading.

We all have our own destinations designed by the Master. If we truly want to go in the direction He has for us, we must get His thoughts before we start our day. We must be still to hear His voice.

So, today as you walk your seashore of life, find that quiet place where you can hear the voice of God. He is waiting to speak to you, to give you direction and to give you wisdom for your walk. He has your destinations mapped out for you if you can hear what He is saying to you.

> *I will instruct you and teach you in the way you should go;*
> *I will counsel you and watch over you.*
>
> — *Psalm 32:8*

As I walked the seaside with Jesus, my heart was overflowing with gratitude for the beauty of the day and the cool air to breathe! The beauty of His creation surrounded me everywhere I looked. What a perfect day to offer sacrifices of praise and gratitude.

What about you, my friend? Are you grateful for all He has given you to enjoy? Have you ever considered perhaps you are not getting your prayers answered because you are not grateful for what God already has done for you? The Scriptures teach us we should continually give God thanks. We always should live with an attitude of gratitude.

You may say, "I've been through so many disappointments. I lost my business last year. My relationship didn't work. My children are not following God." If it had not been for the goodness of God, you could have lost it all. If it were not for God's mercy, you might not even be here today.

So, today as you walk your seashore of life, start thanking God for what you have today to enjoy—for the things He already has manifested in your life. I promise you will find things for which to be grateful. Rise up. Be a threat to the enemy by being who God has called you to be! You are the conqueror. You are the victor over every circumstance in life!

*It is good to praise the LORD and make music to your name,
O Most High, to proclaim your love in the morning
and your faithfulness at night.*

— *Psalm 92:1-2*

As I walked the seaside with Jesus, the beauty of the beach was covered by a cold, gray sky. But the real beauty of the beach was there, no matter how the gray sky masked it.

I thought of how we sometimes wear masks as Christians... afraid to be who we really are, trying to please others. Are you tired of playing games, wearing masks and trying to be someone other than who you are? Wouldn't you like the freedom to just be accepted as you are, without pressure to be someone you really don't know how to be? Would you like to learn how to succeed at being yourself?

God wants you to accept yourself, to like who you are and to learn to deal with your weaknesses. Everyone has weaknesses, but God doesn't want you to reject yourself because of them. If you base your value on your weaknesses, you will underestimate your worth. Your worth is not based on anything you do but on what God already has done for you.

So, today as you walk your seashore of life, if the devil has been trying to convince you that you don't measure up to the proper standard, remind him that everyone is imperfect. God loves you just the way you are.

> *In the same way, the Spirit helps us in our weakness. We do not know what we ought to pray for, but the Spirit himself intercedes for us with groans that words cannot express.*
>
> — *Romans 8:26*

As I walked the seaside with Jesus, I watched as one of the fishermen on the beach had caught a baby shark and was working furiously to take the hook out of its mouth, trying to free him. But the baby shark was wrestling with him, causing the shark more pain, as the fisherman was trying to set him free. Finally, the hook was out, and the baby shark swam swiftly back to the freedom of the sea.

So many times when God is wrestling with us to free us from our pain and trouble, we fight Him in the release. Does this sound familiar to you? It certainly has been true in my own life—when I would find myself in trouble and try to get myself out with my own devices! I could hear God saying, "this is the way out." But, I would continue to fight His ways, going my own rebellious ways and trying to find other solutions. It would have been so much easier and quicker if only I had let the Master free me from the pain I had created.

Do you believe God is there waiting to rescue you from the troubles of the world? He says in His Word if we only will call on Him, He will rescue us out of all our troubles. He does not lie. So, today as you walk your seashore of life, let Him rescue you out of all your troubles, and walk peacefully through the storms of life. He is waiting for you!

> *May the LORD answer you when you are in distress;*
> *may the name of the God of Jacob protect you.*
>
> *— Psalm 20:1*

As I walked the seaside with Jesus, the ocean waves were high and pounding the sand furiously! I wanted to feel calm in my spirit. I wanted evidence all things were calm, but I only saw the fury of the ocean.

Count on it. There will be days when you will want evidence that God is still actively providing what He has promised you. The details of how He is working everything out is what will concern you the most.

Your faith grows by releasing all the particulars to His care. Do not fear. He has taken every facet into account and will use every hurdle to display His power. God always provides for those who love and do as He says. Instead of fearing the lean days, rejoice that His provision never ends.

So, today as you walk your seashore of life, be assured God has considered, and taken care of, details that never entered your mind. You don't have to lose hope as long as you believe in Him. You only have to trust Him. Soon enough the proof will be before you—your faith has not been in vain.

> Then he said: "Praise be to the LORD, the God of Israel, who with his own hand has fulfilled what he promised with his own mouth to my father David...."
>
> — *1 Kings 8:15*

As I walked the seaside with Jesus, I thanked God for the incredible opportunities He has given me in this life. There is an amazing benefit to meditating on all God has done. Dwell on His goodness and it truly will inspire you. Recall His excellent words, and your faith continually will be renewed. Express your appreciation for His provision, your trust in His flawless character and your heart will soar to the threshold of Heaven.

Are you thankful for the blessings in your life, or are you frustrated with the small scope of your lot? Do you wish for opportunities of greater influence, responsibility and reward?

Your present situation may be limited. God, however, has given it as an investment in your future. If you were to have all the success you desire, you may find yourself ill-equipped to handle it. Even worse, you may miss the greatest gift of all—a loving and fulfilling relationship with your Heavenly Father.

In your current circumstances, God is able to teach you what truly is valuable and build the character necessary for the success He has planned for you. Therefore, faithfully invest yourself in whatever He gives you. Soon He will trust you with even greater opportunities.

So, today as you walk your seashore of life, be thankful. Know the Father has incredible success planned for you. He knows exactly when you are ready to receive all that is yours.

> *"Whoever can be trusted with very little can also be trusted with much, and whoever is dishonest with very little will also be dishonest with much."*
>
> *— Luke 16:10*

$\mathcal{A}$s I walked the seaside with Jesus, my mind reflected on the amazing sunrises He creates. I was captivated by the appearance of the sun as it slowly rose above the ocean creating a breathtaking new day, every day.

As I watched this take place, I thought of how we, as believers in Jesus Christ, are all citizens of spiritual light. You no longer need to hide yourself or your actions in darkness where there is no real armor, only the constant threat of being revealed. Because of the brightness God has given you, your impenetrable protection now comes from faith and love.

Think in terms of the campaigns you encounter on a daily basis. You do not have to rely on covert strategies in order to advance to victory. It is your trust in God, and how you care for others, that exalts you. Wherever you are on the path of life, whatever you are going through, look for the beauty in it. God knows the path from beginning to end, and He will make it lovely.

So, today as you walk your seashore of life, embrace the new rules of engagement. Concentrate on shining goodness into the lives of other people. Become the sunrise for those who are in darkness. Let your light shine brighter each day—just as the sun shines brighter the higher it gets into the sky. Be the light in a dark world for everyone you meet.

In everything you do, stay away from complaining and arguing, so that no one can speak a word of blame against you. You are to live clean, innocent lives as children of God in a dark world full of crooked and perverse people. Let your lives shine brightly before them. Hold tightly to the word of life, so that when Christ returns, I will be proud that I did not lose the race and that my work was not useless.

— *Philippians 2:14-16 (NLT)*

As I walked the seaside with Jesus, I noticed how all the creatures seem to work together... the sea gulls, the sandpipers, the pelicans... never worrying about what the others are doing or have done. What a wonderful way to live with one another.

I then thought about how we interact with each other in today's culture. We always seem to be comparing ourselves to others or worrying about the wrongs we have received. It seems it is easier for people to believe negative facts than positive ones—always to remember the wrong that has been done, rather than the good.

This is absolutely not true with God. When you believe in Him, He promises to competely erase any instance where you have fallen short. He remembers and celebrates all the good works you have done out of love.

Do you feel at times as if God has forgotten you? God neither has forgotten you nor the ways you have served Him throughout your life. So, today as you walk your seashore of life, just rejoice that the thoughts He has toward you are—and will always be—outstanding!

> *God is not unjust; he will not forget your work and the love you have shown him as you have helped his people and continue to help them.*
>
> *— Hebrews 6:10*

As I walked the seaside with Jesus, I always dressed comfortably to enjoy my walk with Him. On this particular day it was late, and I was tired—ready for the sunset of the day.

What will you put on when you lie down to go to sleep? Do you have some old, favorite pajamas you sleep in at night? The clothes you put on to rest in at night are generally your most comfortable.

Likewise, dress your mind for bed by removing the concerns of the day and wrapping your thoughts in the calming truth that God delights in you. The One Who protects you does not sleep but tenderly guards you throughout the night.

Before you finally drift off to dreamland, let Him know how much you appreciate His gentle vigilance. Praise Him for the secure comfort that will warm you as you slumber and will faithfully cover you tomorrow. As you end each day, know He has you covered with His love and protection.

> *I will lie down and sleep in peace, for you alone,*
> *O LORD, make me dwell in safety.*
>
> — *Psalm 4:8*

As I walked the seaside with Jesus, I saw several little sandpipers sitting on the ground asleep. This is not normal for them. Usually they are quickly running along the beach, but today, they were sleeping.

I thought about us in our Christian walk. Are we sleeping when we need to be wide awake and praying? When Jesus took the disciples to Gethsemane, He wanted them to keep watch and pray with Him, but they kept falling asleep. He was trying to prepare them for the trial that was coming. As Jesus prayed, an angel came and strengthened Him in spirit which enabled Him to endure the Cross.

Our spirits are willing to do what is right, but our flesh will not help us. Our flesh will rule us if we don't pray. We must ask God to strengthen us in spirit and to help us resist the temptations we may encounter each day.

So, today as you walk your seashore of life, although your flesh may be tired, take time each day to spend in prayer. Be prepared for whatever comes your way tomorrow. Be built up in the spirit! God has gone before us and we must follow!

> *"Watch and pray so that you will not fall into temptation. The spirit is willing, but the body is weak."*
>
> — *Matthew 26:41*

As I walked the seaside with Jesus, I realized how easy it is to enjoy the world around us when we walk with the attitude of Christ. It is amazing how God changes your attitude toward everything as you walk with Him.

It is an astounding thing, indeed, when God's wisdom finally makes sense to you. The issues, the people and the circumstances that brought you pain begin to be transformed into vessels of good. These changes teach you to look for God's excellent purposes, in even the most insignificant occurrences, knowing they may hold some instructive glimpse of His character.

Be strong, be encouraged and prevail like the soldier assured of triumph. Be firm and secure in your hope. Resolutely prepare yourself for the victory He is bringing you. Take heart—whenever your heart fails you, or you are fearful regarding your circumstances—allow Him to support you. Exhibit determination, and experience His courage as it pulses throughout your inner being, emboldening your will, mind and soul.

So, today as you walk your seashore of life, you may not be at the place where you can say God intended some difficult thing for good. Be encouraged that the transformation He makes in you is truly worthwhile. Wait for the Lord. He is coming to you in strength and glory.

> *"You intended to harm me, but God intended it for good to accomplish what is now being done, the saving of many lives."*
>
> — *Genesis 50:20*

As I walked the seaside with Jesus, many thanks went to my Father Who has given me the privilege of walking in such peace daily along the shore of the beautiful ocean.

I think of the world we live in—a world of chaos and unrest. People in the world are under such intense pressure. They are often hurried, rude, short-tempered and frustrated. They experience financial and marital stress, and the stress of raising children, in a changing and uncertain world. Because of mental stress on the job, and physical stress from overwork and frayed nerves, some people seem to be time bombs on the verge of explosion.

As a believer, you do not need to succumb to the stress that affects people who do not know Jesus as their Savior. You do not have to operate in the world's system. God has given you a better way to live. God has provided ways for you to live in the world without being affected by that type of stress.

So, today as you walk your seashore of life, remember, Jesus is the Prince of Peace. Following the leading of the Holy Spirit always will lead you to peace and joy—not to anxiety and frustration.

> *"I have given them your word and the world has hated them,*
> *for they are not of the world any more than I am of the world.*
> *My prayer is not that you take them out of the world*
> *but that you protect them from the evil one."*
>
> *— John 17:14-15*

As I walked the seaside with Jesus, the sand was piled in batches from the storm that had washed up on the beach overnight. The beach was more erupted than usual... just as our lives sometimes become from the daily storms that seem to overtake us.

I am reminded how Jesus told Peter to keep his eyes on Him as Peter walked toward Jesus on the water. Peter was fine until he took his eyes off Jesus. Then Peter was overcome by the waves of the ocean. That is where we go wrong. We take our eyes off Jesus and begin to look at the circumstances around us. We then become distracted, unfocused and unable to move forward because of the worries and fears of the storms we face. Our personal storms become bigger than any natural storm our Father would create.

You may be trying hard to make things work right but are still failing. Your problem is not that you are a failure. Your problem is simply that you have not gone to the right source for help... your Heavenly Father.

So, today as you walk your seashore of life, keep your eyes on Jesus, not on the storms around you. He will keep you walking above the waves of life. He is there with His hand extended to hold you. Walk toward Him and keep your peace! Stay focused and overcome!

He got up, rebuked the wind and said to the waves, "Quiet! Be still!" Then the wind died down and it was completely calm.

— Mark 4:39

As I walked the seaside with Jesus, a young girl needed help with her beach chair. I stopped to help her get it set up and went on my way. God reminded me we always should be prompt to meet a need when we see it.

When God tells you to help someone, it is easy to put it off. You intend to obey God, but you are going to do it later—when you have more money, when you're not so busy, when the kids are back in school or when vacation is over. There is no point in praying for God to give you money, so you can be a blessing to others, if you are not being a blessing with what you already have.

Satan will try to tell you that you don't have anything to give—but don't believe him. Even if it is only small amounts of money, a pack of gum, a ballpoint pen or a few minutes of your time, start using what you have. As you begin to give what you have, God will bring increase. You then will be able to give in a greater way.

We must always remember we are His ambassadors on the earth. Others see Jesus by how we, His followers, love them and give of ourselves to them. The Shepherd cares for His flock every moment. When we follow Him we will do as He does.

So, today as you walk your seashore of life, lend a hand when the opportunity comes your way. Give from what you have, and you will be entrusted with even more to give.

Do not say to your neighbor, "Come back later;
I'll give it tomorrow"—when you now have it with you.

— Proverbs 3:28

$\mathcal{A}$s I walked the seaside with Jesus, I once again was reminded of how much I love His wonderful ocean... a place to listen to sounds that only the waves can make.

I have walked miles along the shoreline, leaving my footprints in the sand, which then are invaded by the endless ebb and flow of the tide. These moments bring me an unspeakable calm. I can see with a clear mind and heart all the ways God has held my life in His hands. He has walked me through the violent storms to bring me to a restful place. Even the bad memories—those painful reminders of hurt and disappointment—somehow get covered with a sweet forgiveness, leaving a yearning for all to be right and true under the warm blanket of the Lord's mercy.

It is when my mind is stayed on Jesus, when my eyes look toward eternal things, when my ears listen way beyond the voices of the day, that I hear the ocean sing. The Lord miraculously puts everything into His perspective when my mind thinks on Him... and Him alone.

So, today as you walk your seashore of life, let your mind be at peace as you meditate on the things your Heavenly Father has done for you! In so doing, true peace will be your strength!

> *May the God of hope fill you with all joy and peace*
> *as you trust in him, so that you may overflow with hope*
> *by the power of the Holy Spirit.*

— *Romans 15:13*

$\mathcal{A}$s I walked the seaside with Jesus, two tiny sandpipers were running together along the sand. They were playing, stopping to look at one another, then off to play again.

As I thought of how God teaches us that two are better than one, I thought of how much stronger we are when we are joined with someone to stand with us, to pray with us... to play with us. Sometimes just their very presence seems to make the situation better and our spirits stronger. When there seems to be no apparent solution at that moment, all it takes is one word from someone to lift our spirits and strengthen us for whatever we may be facing that day!

It is the same way with God. He created man so He could have fellowship with us. He is always with us and never leaves us. We truly are never alone.

So, today as you walk your seashore of life, know that His presence in our lives makes us powerful, with the ability to do all things. He is our ever-present hope and help in this life. We can rejoice knowing He created us to walk together with Him and with others. Be strengthened today, and rejoice in the knowledge you are never alone!

> *Praise be to the Lord, to God our Savior,*
> *who daily bears our burdens. Selah*
>
> — *Psalm 68:19*

$\mathcal{A}$s I walked the seaside with Jesus, I watched the schools of fish jumping out of the water in abundance! I had seen one or two at a time jump, but this day they were jumping on every wave. The pelicans were having a feast!

We have that same abundance available to us. It is from our Father in Heaven. He is decreeing and declaring abundance for us at all times. Even those times when the world seems to be moving in "lack," His children can live and move in "abundance."

We are His children, and He is not going to withhold any good thing from us. We can focus on what the world is saying—the voice of the media and those who are in fear—or we can focus on what our Father in Heaven is saying!

God already has equipped you with everything you need to live a prosperous life and to fulfill your God-given destiny. He planted "seeds" inside you filled with possibilities, incredible potential, creative ideas and dreams. However, you have to start planting those seeds in fertile soil before you can reap a harvest.

So, today as you walk your seashore of life, go to your Father in Heaven; tell Him your needs. Stand in faith—believing God will do what He says He will do. He will meet your needs—even more than you can ask or think! He is El Shaddai. He is more than enough!

> *And my God will meet all your needs according to his glorious riches in Christ Jesus.*
>
> — *Philippians 4:19*

As I walked the seaside with Jesus, the ocean sparkled like diamonds; the sand was as smooth as silk; the flowers and palms were brilliant with the glory of the sun shining through their leaves. Everything was so pristine; it made me think of how Heaven will be.

When I see the beauty we have to enjoy on this earth, it is almost hard to fathom the beauty we will experience in Heaven. But oh, how much more glorious it will be! God has promised that Heaven will be more glorious than anything we can imagine here on earth. Heaven is going to be so overwhelming when we see it!

At times I try to imagine what our Father has promised for those who follow Him to Heaven. He has given us a promise of life and glory with Him full of beauty and peace. The beauty, the glory, the peace…. Who would want to risk missing that? His Word says He has prepared these things for us. Let's never stray from the path He is showing us.

So, today as you walk your seashore of life, know nothing we have can compare to what is to come. Be ready for Him to come for us any day! You don't want to miss it!

"In my Father's house are many rooms; if it were not so, I would have told you. I am going there to prepare a place for you. And if I go and prepare a place for you, I will come back and take you to be with me that you also may be where I am."

— John 14:2-3

As I walked the seaside with Jesus, the sun had risen and seemed brighter than other days. It was as if the glory of God was shining through the clouds and being magnified as it glistened on the water.

When Moses returned from meeting with God on Mount Sinai, his face shone so brightly, it astonished the Israelites. Such was the result of being in God's presence—the brilliance of God lingered on the countenance of Moses.

Are you making time for God? Are you scurrying about, accomplishing tasks that in the end will be meaningless? Speak to your Heavenly Father. Spend time with Him each day. Let Him order your steps. He will make your time more meaningful and more productive in this thing called "life."

Though your time with God may be somewhat different than Moses', the lasting effect, nevertheless, will be the same. God's glory will show through you. Although you may not notice any difference when looking in the mirror, others will see the glow of His likeness in your spirit and character.

Every time you meet with God, it will affect you in a positive way. So, today as you walk your seashore of life, spend time with Him. Let the beauty of His radiance shine through you.

> *Those who look to him are radiant;*
> *their faces are never covered with shame.*

— *Psalm 34:5*

As I walked the seaside with Jesus, I helped a little fish find his way back into the water. He was gasping for air and once again was filled with life as he escaped the dry beach that had overtaken him. He had gotten out of the safety zone of the water.

Psalm 81 was written in celebration of Israel's miraculous deliverance from Egypt. It is a reminder that God's powerful provision is always available for His people, but we must obey Him to fully see His hand touch our situation.

You may be tempted to disregard God and handle your situations and troubles on your own. But remember, whenever the people of Israel did that, they progressively got into more trouble. They kept getting farther away from the land God promised He had for them. Only when the Israelites trusted God and obeyed Him did they finally enter the Promised Land.

What needs do you have today? Are you trying to handle them on your own? Remember, you are not alone in your struggles. You have the God of the Universe Who loves you and is ready to bring the victory to you! Turn your battles over to Him, and watch what He does. God will help you, and provide for you, if you will humble yourself and admit you need Him. He has exactly what you need. Let Him lead you into the Promised Land.

> *"I am the LORD your God, who brought you up out of Egypt. Open wide your mouth and I will fill it."*
>
> — *Psalm 81:10*

$\mathcal{A}$s I walked the seaside with Jesus, I felt the love of my Father holding my hand as we walked together. I was reminded of the commandment to love the Lord God with all our hearts, souls and strength.

If God told us to do this, He made provision to give us the will and ability to do it! As we love our Father, He will give us the ability to love others. Just walk in His love daily—what a simple way to live in a world where love is not always found.

Think of the way you love others. Do you love them if they are perfect, pretty or successful? Do you love them because they deserve to be loved or because we are commanded to love them? Think of how you love others. Compare it to the way your Father in Heaven loves you. Does He love you because you are perfect, pretty or successful? No. He loves you because God is love. His love flows through us, perfecting us, and then flows to others. His love helps us survive every challenge and gives meaning to our lives.

So, today as you walk your seashore of life, determine to love God with all your heart. Reach outside of yourself, and love those around you with the love of the Father. You then will be able to see His love abound in every area of your life! His commandment is for us to love one another as He loves us!

> *Jesus replied: "Love the Lord your God with all your heart and with all your soul and with all your mind.'"*
>
> — *Matthew 22:37*

As I walked the seaside with Jesus, I kept looking back to see where I had been and how far I had walked. I don't seem to cover as much territory looking back as I do staying focused and moving forward.

"There is a time for everything... a time to weep and a time to laugh, a time to mourn and a time to dance" (Ecclesiastes 3:1, 4). You would be cold hearted and lacking compassion if you experienced loss and felt nothing. But after a while, you must let go of what lies behind, and press forward. If you don't, the past will destroy your future.

God told Joshua, "'Moses my servant is dead. Now then, you and all these people, get ready to cross the Jordan River into the land I am about to give to them—to the Israelites. I will give you every place where you set your foot, as I promised Moses'" (Joshua 1:2-3). Like the children of Israel, God wants you to let go of the past, and take new ground. Don't spend the rest of your life mourning something you have lost.

So, today as you walk your seashore of life, look forward to the future—don't look back. What is back there has already happened. Looking back will not change it. Look forward to what is to come. Your journey is not yet over. Learn from your past mistakes and regrets. Move forward with hope and assurance that God wants to give you the desires of your heart with joy in the morning.

For his anger lasts only a moment, but his favor lasts a lifetime; weeping may remain for a night, but rejoicing comes in the morning.

— *Psalm 30:5*

$\mathcal{A}$s I walked the seaside with Jesus, He reminded me that today many are led astray because they do not know the truth about life. Truth is the only thing that will set us free to live life with joy as God planned for us.

Today, we hear many excuses for living otherwise—everybody is doing it; do unto others before they do it unto you; if I didn't have bad luck, I would have no luck at all. All of these excuses are keeping us from living a life of truth.

You will never hear words of excuse coming from God. Excuses keep you from being accountable to yourself and to those around you. You need to know the truth, and be true to yourself. It is the only way you will ever make a difference in this world where you live!

Make it your goal to seek the truth about life. Take time to be with the Father, and read His Word. He will show you the true way you are to live. You cannot live a balanced life unless you face the truth of who you are and what God says about you. This is the only way to be free!

So, today as you walk your seashore of life, become a warrior for the truth! A warrior's belief is constantly being aligned with the truth! Warriors will always know where they stand in life! Become a warrior for truth today. Be free!

"Then you will know the truth, and the truth will set you free."

— John 8:32